T0282198

DEBRIS

Also by Jonathan Wells

Train Dance
The Man with Many Pens

DEBRIS

Jonathan Wells

Four Way Books
Tribeca

Library of Congress Cataloging-in-Publication Data

Names: Wells, Jonathan, author.
Title: Debris / Jonathan Wells.
Description: New York : Four Way Books, [2021] | Includes bibliographical
references. | Identifiers: LCCN 2020038075 |
ISBN 9781945588716 (trade paperback)
Subjects: LCGFT: Poetry.
Classification: LCC PS3623.E4695 D43 2021 | DDC 811/.6--dc23
LC record available at https://lccn.loc.gov/2020038075

This book is manufactured in the United States of America and printed on
acid-free paper.

Four Way Books is a not-for-profit literary press. We are grateful for the assistance
we receive from individual donors, public arts agencies, and private foundations.

This publication is made possible with public funds from the
New York State Council on the Arts, a state agency.

We are a proud member of the Community of Literary Magazines and Presses.

Contents

Notes

Let your pure
space crowd my heart,
that we might stay awhile longer amid the
flying debris.

This, Twice Removed
Ralph Angel (1951-2020)

POMPEII

Each language is a dream
of language, a way of seeing
the buried, ethereal city,
of saying what you've seen.

It lodges beyond memory,
entire, intact, as whole as Hera
who rushes out and bolts
in a flash like a moment
you may not remember.

NOTES FROM THE INVASION
for Christopher Merrill

The worst has happened. There is nothing
to imagine. Guards are posted at the gates
of the city. Their leader is a thief. He rises
and all stand for him. He doffs his hat
and they bow their heads.

We have surrendered our papers to the sad-
faced lieutenant. Now we are abandoned
to our bodies and the thin shellac of rain
on the vacant pavements.

The protests will begin later. Or never.
The chants will bounce off the facades
of empty buildings. Scaffolds will rattle
on their stanchions. There is no light
but a shadow in the hallway. A beggar's
hand was a closed fist until it was hungry.

There is nothing to imagine. The worst
has happened and the streets are slick.

LIVING IN THE POEM

He moves into the poem
as if it were a fortress
in a field of wild azalea.
The walls are close. He reaches
out and touches the ironwood.
There are wavy glass windows
and night is barely lit but
bright enough for words.

The floor is made of pebbles
and dirt that smells of rain.
It's crossed by ragged lines
of ants carrying crumbs
twenty times their size.
That's what most work is
hauling food from here to
there, storing it in mounds.

He shapes a chimney with his hands
as if it were a clay vessel rising
on a wheel, something tapered

to snake the smoke away.
He strengthens it so no one
could say how long it had
been there. It was always there
standing against the clouds.

CLOUDS ARE PEOPLE TOO!

Some are vapor and scatter
randomly in the sunset.
Others snag the tops of pines
and telephone poles
tumbling up the hills
and culverts.

They travel in gangs.
They quarrel, they shush.
They marvel. They muddy
what the sun picks clean.

They serenade and flash
salmon with ash gray ribs.
Some clouds are spread so thin.

Some are barbarians
and some are thieves.

What does a cloud desire
but its nature; the mood,
the form, the motion.

HOW DID I LOVE MYSELF AGAIN

After the war, I learned to love myself
the old-fashioned way. I took my circus
shirt from the bottom drawer, the one
with clowns and acrobats clapping
for the children. Its rich blue wrapped
around me like a serape.

In that embrace I laughed out loud
and it was a laughter giddier
than the weather. It bowled
through me like tumbleweed
through a Western town when
there was no tempest in the forecast.
It emptied me but didn't leave me hollow.

When there was no one to come home to
I duckwalked through the halls and those
rockabilly chords shocked my solid guitar
body. I could feel myself loosen at the neck.
My spine unlocked and I rocked back
and forth almost dancing, not waiting
for someone to tap me on the shoulder.

The porch greeted me without hailstones.
Broken leaves cascaded from the beams.
I was hatless and they mixed into my hair
like herbs. I lowered my sweet, infected
head and the current whooshed over me.
Like luck. Like a breeze from nowhere.

FANDANGO

The dancer in her first or final dance
steps in and out of the disco lights.

No heart, the bullet craves her heart.
No blood, the bullet craves her blood,

idle air, her mind in flight, what
guides her feet.

Desire is a tight, shrunken map
where lovers carve their common dance.

THE SEVENTH DAY

On the seventh day God made nothing—
not peace or patience or love or kindness
but the day was still holy.

The sun rose without urgency or heat.
Waves flashed a mackerel silver.
God agitated in the bed of the world
and there was a twitch of thunder
in the hills.

A class of lesser gods complained
that he was lazy. There was so much
left undone. What about the heart's
refinement, they asked. What is
the body's perfection worth if
the mind was cored? A forest
without a cave?

God ignored them. Their questions
had no purpose. What he made
he made perfect. Completion
was not his mission. The brain
was curious enough and agile. The senses
could be trusted. What more could be

done for them? How was the father good
who gave his children everything?

He told them he could love anyone
but love was a misnomer.
His was not a mother's love where
any infraction might be forgiven.
Their mistakes were hideous.
They must solve their own mistakes.
His love is not eternal.
It was a spasm,
a flirtation. Now he is
tired. Let him rest.

TAKING OFF THE VEST

I didn't want to kill anyone, Aisha said.

Who are you? the guard asked. *Did they send you
to murder me?*

I came here on my own.

Come closer, the old man said and leaned
    his rifle against the acacia tree. *The grass
is high. No one will see us here. Stretch out
    your arms slowly.*

*I'm sorry my scarf is soiled. They wouldn't let
    me wash it. I am scared.*

*If they only knew how big your courage was
    they would fight to wash your feet,*
he said and unhooked the transistor radio's clasp.

She shivered in the elephant grass
    until she heard the blast that shook
the ground. Then the world was quiet
    again and she wondered how
the savannah birds could still sing.

13

YOUR HAT

Your hat is shouting at me.
Its sequins are flashing
like caution lights. Its cone
is a megaphone.

Please ask it to be quiet.
It is distracting me
from what I was feeling.

Your angora sweater, a shade
of cantaloupe, is bursting
into flames. It blazes through
my overcoat and singes
my fingertips. Please douse.
My hand is so gnarled
that soon I won't be able
to hold my morning cup
of coffee.

The sun advises me to be steady.
I was silent steadily until
your hat approached me.
Can you hear me, it keeps asking.

I love answering your questions
but I hate myself for listening.
Please don't interrupt me while
I linger for every word you say.

SIX LIVES

I lived six lives not end to end
but blended in one life
like the man baking a kugel
pudding that the heat pulled in
as he backed away from the oven.
Its waves clawed at him. A baker
man, a better man than he'd have
been had he been left alone.

In another column, I was also me.
My bones were wrapped in burlap
like little shoots struggling for life.
Sometimes I blossomed.
Sometimes I was thirsty
when I surprised myself
in the mirror
like a tall building
caught in copper by sunrise,
the upward light.

I told six true stories I couldn't feel
until the latches clicked into place
and then I heard them lift.
My chest gave out, my red shirt

popped its buttons and smoke
wafted out of me.

It was a chilly day. My boots were
a yellow leather. My coat was gray.
We walked together and no one
saw how many walked with me.

DEBRIS

After the storm I picked up sticks
doing what my father did
on Saturdays. I heaped them
in a shaky pile that teetered
and began to slip, kindling
for a fire to warm the afternoon.

When he'd asked me to come with him
I'd refused but watched him stoop
from the warm side of the window.
The bundle grew under his arm
as he crossed the lawn carrying
load after load to the lower

ground where he let me strike
the match in spite of my recusal.

GLASS TABLE

Sorry for my feet.
They are knobbly
and a little purple
around the ankles.
Prankster feet,
feet that waltzed
and never waltzed.

Untaught,
they had their antic
sway, stop and start
cadence of those
puzzled by what
their movement was
and how it carries
across the day.

TWENTY DOLLAR PEACH

Winter poor, I'm living on fumes but
nothing says fresh money like Spring.
Cherry trees blossom into wads of cash,
wrinkled, pink, fragrant in memory.
New green buds burst on branches
like the bills of my small savings.
Even the iris sports a blue silk
ascot at the throat of its stalk.

This fortune I save for another season;
to hoard for parched summer, to splurge
on the sweetest, ripest peach, to swirl
in the ecstasy of its nectar, a payment
that rescues me from thirst, springs me
from the ruin of the first autumn rain.

Let us go freely now that the night
is succulent and clear and the breeze
buoyant. We'll sail through tollbooths
shuttered on parkways that are always
open, stretched out before us
like Möbius strips untwisted
into endless miles of pavement.
Those fumes will be our feet.

STAY

My reasons for not loving launch
their familiar cries. I blame the sun

for its blanket light, the moon for being
too bright. I blame my sight for noticing

too late that my hands are holding
her away. It is she who should speak first

I hear myself say. It is she who should
say love. It was not my turn to speak.

If she were bolder, I could
accept a smile that is

too brief for pleasure, a caress
that is too light for solace.

Pardon the day that told me
she was right to go, the hours

she spent away. Stay.

BREATHING INTO THE BOOK: *THE ASIATICS*

Standing on the shore of Istanbul
Mr. Suleiman hands me a satchel
filled with opium.

I inhale the page's fragrance and complete
the scene; gulet heavy in the water,
streetlamps at dusk along the harbor,
the satchel's cloying aroma.

He told me I should throw it
in the water near the buoy
when the boat reaches Trebizond.
An Egyptian will retrieve it
and take it to the city.

I breathe into the book
and forget that I am breathing.

All of this he'd said a hundred times
before but never to an American.
He handed me the package
and told me "Be loyal and Brave,
my young American. Remember,"
he said, "to always be afraid."

I breathe into the alphabet.
I breathe into the book and forget
that I am reading. The book
exhales a breath of pulp.
I breathe as if I'm sleeping.
I breathe as if I'm hiding
in a deep forest but I know
that they still look for me.

BETRAYAL

America, we let you sleep too late.
You wake up groggy and confused
not recognizing the bedroom curtains.
You rise anyway, slick your hair back.
Your fingers claw the banister,
your knees buckle on the stairs.

We are your children and follow your descent
agape. Your mouth is parched so drink
of us to soothe your throat. We are
your holy water, your vitamins, your
morning pill. Without us, there is
no roof, no house, no bedrock stairs.

CHELSEA BOMBING

1.

First there was the magnesium flash
of sparks, then the spewed lightning;
bolts, screws, and wires fanning out
from an unknown source. The victims,

maimed and bleeding, running still,
were hoisted and dropped down
like debris the sky rains after
an explosion. And then there was

my conceit that this time the blast
was worse because it was merely
blocks away, not continents or days.
Our windows rattled with the news

that came in reverb waves and echoes:
random act, demented warrior, God's
conscript, divine belief. I fidgeted in
my bed, not shouldering the lame.

2.

His body curved on the pavement. Was he
asleep? His forearm wrapped in gauze
served as a shimmy for his head. The scene
was shrouded in mist with a passing lick
of rain. He had been human once
before he fell.

His father denounced him as a terrorist
and said he'd turned sour. His sister
recanted his stabbing of her leg. He worked
the fat fryer at First American Fried Chicken
before he fell.

His co-workers said he'd grown silent
but it wasn't the silence of angels, it was
the silence of living upside down, in cacophony,
cowering in an echo chamber of curses
and vows unraveling that only dynamite
could drown out.

Pissed himself on a doorsill, he reeked
of disappointment, the solace of heaven
shattered like a snow globe on the sidewalk,
dishevelment another sign of his impatience
for deliverance to what was holy.

3.

The city grid was rotated twenty-nine degrees
clockwise to true West so the sun nested in the cleavage
of buildings at the end of twenty-third street.
Once burly stones now glossed to slab
their sleek skin carried a faint rose sheen
mirroring the river and the solstice evening.

Manhattanhenge. Midsummer barged past us.
The year tilted toward its shrinking. He was
a terrorist and we were victims. We were
terrorists and he was a victim. Distinctions
boiled off and the broad street flowed
back and forth from river to river, end to end.

THE THIRTEENTH LABOR

For Hercules, the thirteenth labor,
    is allowing the mortal lovers to go
back to their separate beds unreconciled,
    to leave well enough alone,
        to let their oaths uncouple
from their stars, to abandon the
            strange planets
      to the idiosyncrasies of their orbits.

    To shun the power that Zeus
had given, Hercules searches for fortitude
    along an ordinary shore where all waves
reach their breaking point, some staring
    with demonic eyes
        while others lap
the beach rhapsodically.

    Recovering, he asks
the heavens for extra strength, not sleight
       of hand or muscles he'd flexed before
cleaning or slaughtering or filching

the golden apples of the nymphs.
     He prays for
a mind that would leave the lovers
        alone with their distrust.

   But that is another fantasy
of self-possession, of holding himself in check,
        letting love be love; love refused, or
     breathing lightly or unloved
        like unpicked apples. The lovers' slurs,
staccato, strike the night and he is
      certain that turning away
   is his one impossible labor.

HIS FIRST MOOSE

A hillside looms behind him,
a relief of silhouettes.
In the crater valley
the moon is half a walnut shell,
a fragment of a halo.

The moose lowers her crown of antlers
and paws the sandy ground. She senses
that he's there and ruts against the bark
to block his body, one bloodshot eye
alert to the briefest motion.

I am not a hunter, he offers.
No rifle or bullets or aim to menace.
I hiked up this morning,
for a broader view of the valley.
She moves sideways but doesn't stray.

Both have palisades of safety
to retreat to where they take
their shelter, a refuge not a fortress
even if the trail is narrow
along the ridge and the path
is mostly sky.

ODE TO THE POST OFFICE

The clock isn't ticking.
The lines are long and time is
missing. We brace ourselves
against the counters as if we are
balancing on an iceberg that is barely
floating the way streets stay
flat while the earth is curving.

Men clutch the fragile parcels
of their earnings. May they arrive
unbroken. Mothers clutch baby shoes
wrapped in tissue. May they fit
those crumpled feet. The walls
are padded with envelopes
and cardboard boxes. The light
is simple this far from the sun.

A bodiless hand reaches
through plexiglass to receive
the package. Some mouth
an inaudible prayer.

A woman leans on a counter
as though she were kneeling
in her pew. Apostolic
Church of Solace.

The world is suspended in magic
like a birdcage lined with trinkets;
windchimes that tinkle
when the gate slides open,
slots, stamps like holy tokens,
pens on musical chains, paperclips,
stickers and labels. Slowness
is contagious.

Patron saint of travelers waiting
at the crossing, Saint Christopher slouches
through the hall in a blue postman's suit.

ONE GARDEN

We are wandering separate paths
next to the ocean. You wave to me

from the half-moon bridge. I wave back.
Love is the answer to love that wavers.

You stop at a Japanese stone lantern
and caress the brownish moss.

A boy spreads his arms standing
under the limbs of a giant banyan tree

as if he were receiving an ovation.
Leaves shake with giddy exultation.

The fisherman unbaits his hook
and stops to watch the yellow

helmet bird stand in midair
for an instant before it darts

across the pond pumping
toward the ocean. A man

sitting in his pickup truck
leans out the window as he rolls

a joint from reefer shake.
He strikes a match, exhales

a cloud and soon all of us are high.

PAGE ONE

Before the book opens, the plotting
is yours. The fiction is only you.
When the airplane lifts into the sun,
you are still on page one. But then,
you are rewritten, recrafted,
seized by a foreign language,
the susurrus of other voices.

The flyer becomes the flight.
A fly garnishes the wall.
You turn the page and climb
as the atmosphere consumes you.
The sun is peach on your skyward
cheek. This is how you fly into
the clouds of your unbecoming
where you have no given name.

PARAMOUR

Night parachutes down
like a black snow mistress.
She is that quiet. I part her hair
and whisper *It's Jonathan,*
as if she didn't know me.
She pins my shoulders
to the pillow and asks,

What are you asking?
Didn't I already forgive you?

Her blouse billows over me.
She is supple and strong.
Her long finger presses
against my lips. This is how
I confide in her and we make
our accommodations.

I mutter what I haven't allowed
myself to imagine, how I'd followed
the white heron that flew and flew
with the volition of the river.

Lover of dark tinsel spaces,
sparkling moon fence posts,
she leans over my sheathed body,
her fragrant lanes bordered with black tulips,
her hands like dark ribbons.

If I forgive you again
will you believe me
this time or are you only
calling for my attention?

NOVEMBER 31

Freedom was declared again
on the outer islands and the towns
along the river. A strange freedom,
a freedom that had been granted once.
Freedom to breathe and wander.
They who might have been born
in any town searched for it again.

They shuffled near the ferry selling
loosies, their t-shirts stained yellow.
They were theirs to hawk. It was hard
to breathe that woolen air.

They clutched the cheroots they bought
at the tobacco shop. They were theirs
to hawk. Their smokes were their smokes,
their shaky hands were their only hands.

They dedicate this extra autumn day
to their right to scuff their heels along
the pavement, to blow smoke into
the oak leaves and follow the moon
around the corner.

Each day shrinks to make a place for it.
The earth must stretch around its orbit.
Add it back into the calendar to stand
for those who've vanished, a minute
for every life that was unwritten.

HOUSE OF HOUSES

In the middle of the night the banshees wail
their high-pitched tunes through attic boards.
The house settles deeper in its origins. House
of houses, crossed layers of beam, sunk in a

scattering of brown pine needles. They
began five years ago. Before they came I could
still hear the chatter of old leaves, a hollow
sound or the river running through a sieve

of stones. Voluminous or thin, the river rang.
Whose voices were those? The wind boxed in?
Animals of the afterlife humming their eerie
songs? Spectral squirrels. The mice's tales.

I listened to their voices chortle, sopranos
of the unknown, ravishing and pure like
secret writing that reappears to tell how far
they came and what their lives had been.

AFTER THE VOLCANO

We built our new house
in a field of lava.
Black pumice lawn.

The land was cheap. Streams
in the hills ran magma red.
Runoff steamed the angelfish.

An aftershock left the air
placid yet stale. The sun
greened in the palm's brain.

The fronds lightly shook. Night
passed so fast there wasn't time
to sift the stars dimmed

by the neighbors' lights.
You woke up, a comet streak,
sweaty, lost, and thrashing.

When you were calm we
heard the smallest sound.
Moth wings on the mirror.

We watched as if a magician's
hand had birthed a pea.
Earth that keeps on giving.

GOOD MORNING

The sun shoots blanks today. There's rain
in the forecast and the cold cuts like the scales
of the sunnies I caught in that distant summer lake.

A lady charges down my hallway as if an idea
had been sparked in her that she didn't know
she had, a glimmer, a vision, or a trip to another
continent, a place she'd never thought of visiting.

Or did the morning feel like an unlikely place,
a journey from where she had begun,
a clearing within her or beyond, where
what she wanted was suddenly revealed
and her light, quick steps on the linoleum
were a beginning for both of us who
conspired in her urgent arrival.

HUDSON RIVER

An unexpected story moves me
toward the window. Is it mine
or the one about how the pylons
crumbled and the planks fell.

Ferries and cruise ships roll
along the river's carpet.
A woman on deck signals
to the sun as if it might see her.
The current uncoils
like a constrictor and
its gleaming skin is blue.

A blizzard lies down in the ditch
of the river, fills the empty pockets
of air. Fresh flakes make each
footprint new, the first brave path
these shoes have taken
through cobwebs of snow.

Night is another river of dark
ripples that settles in its bed.
Sleep beneath the eiderdown.
Hold your head in disbelief

and dream of the fearless steps
you took down to the water.
Were those the river's tears
or yours that wet this bank?

I CATCH MYSELF

1.

I catch the minute hand in the act
of ticking. Time doesn't stand still.
It strikes and pauses the way a deer
stops on a hill, frozen at first until
it springs into forest camouflage,
a dun palette of days and hours.

When the digit flips from six
to seven on the bedside clock,
time presses. It's not unseen,
sanding limestone cliffs to dust.

I watch it next to me. We keep
each other's company, two wheels
turning side by side, a tandem
we'll pedal into the future.

2.

I catch my heart in the act of beating.
It reminds me I'm still breathing.
With a sluggish rhythm that
I'd forgotten was my tempo,
I turn on my heartless side.
Dawn amplifies the echo.

I catch myself in the act of loving
leaning into its axis, the enigma
of its center, fearful of its omens,
despite its penchant for revenge.

I catch myself in a flash of faith
believing in what I hoped for, how
I persisted through its mayhem,
how peace settled for an instant.

THE WIND IS LOOSE

Like a zombie, wind staggers through the city
cold-handed. It disobeys the grid. No angle
is right, no direction a refuge. From the West
doesn't mean that East will protect you.
Every step shivers North. Whichever way
you walk the wind is in your face. Your eyes

are wild with tears. It treats you like a thing,
a missing section of the paper excerpted
for the sky and you are its whim, disposable,
the stubble that needs shaving,
a beanie that's been lifted. You are raised
above yourself, made fine, but closer to

the sun that seeps through you. You look down
not believing that so much land arrays
below you. Now you're smaller than the print
on your separation papers, released quickly
from what you had so recently embraced.

WITNESS

He is the bomber and the bomb.
He surveils the neighborhood.
He squints, wanders, and waits
for nothing beyond himself.

                               Daylight
slices through the sleeves
of the pedestrians as if the sun
had bloomed into blades and pellets
and kept bursting. He watches it
in his lonesome trance.

                          There is a beauty
so lonely that no one notices and so
he wants to mail those letters to say
he is that witness: unmailed letters
like the unspoken confessions of those
who suffer, transmissions from a world
that will split and open like an egg
and inside glows the gilded scene
of our sublime and vengeful streets.

MY NEW SHOES

As soon as I put them on, my shoes
unleash me and we walk from one river
to another, from rain to seedless clouds,
the Seaport docks to the Chelsea Piers,
my soles rolling from heel to toe
in their cushioned beds.

The new me is unalloyed, unfettered, untaken,
careless, saying yes and yes and let us go.
Grit parts my hair a little to the side. Wind mats
my eyelashes and moisture wets my cheek.

Walking my heart is all heat, all energy in its
miracle cadence. In spite of sleet, in spite of cold
and hail and pierced by sunshine, I fill my shoes
as if they didn't cost a nickel and the transverse
miles added up to nothing and went nowhere.

ZENO AND THE BEAUTIFUL WALL

In a room without a roof Zeno, ageless,
gauges half the distance across and
half again and half again. A breeze, full
in itself, delivers the scent of charcoal
smoke through the portico. The villagers
bunch together at the gate as he gathers
his white robe, the next step a postulate.
He moves toward the far wall that shines
with an unreachable light as if it were
the sky itself, impossible and near,
something close he could not touch.

The fig and cedar trees know he will be
as gnarled as they are if he achieves the end.
The hawks ignore him but for Zeno each
step is pure attention across a plane,
space and time beholden to the idea
of motion not motion itself. Is it absurd
to proclaim what distance is: the arrow
never hitting the target when the fletcher
releases the string?

On that far wall he projects the profile
of Parmenides who taught him as a boy
standing on a black sand beach against
the sea. The beacon of his argument.
Behind him, the fields are sparse, filled
with rocks. The hills rise and fall
like hypotheses. The body is a carapace.
Only the mind will reach the wall.

SCAFFOLDING

In the sun we are fresh as mint
but in makeshift tunnels, dust
swarms our shadows. The clatter
of shanty tin, two by fours, steel
bars, men with mallets, assault us.
It stops and starts like a headache
or ostinato. Mineshaft lights blink,
go dark. The fear of swift collapse
clinks as we inch our way forward.

The heavy rain that falls on tin
pings to remind us that we are
also grateful we were protected.
Cotillion thick and breathless,
blossoms detonate beyond us,
begging us to yearn for them.
The afternoon is still alive,
so close we can hear it panting.

BETWEEN VÍZNAR AND ALFACAR

We met on a plain of paper next to a ravine
when the blackbirds looped into the olive trees
at the hour when love isn't postponed by hunger.
Two strangers from opposite towns we stood
next to where his grave should have been
inside a scattering of stones.

I said tell me what will carry me from these
used up trees, the blackbirds, this tract of blood.
Show me the temper of your sun, the solace of
your rain, what your darkness solves. Take me
wherever you can persuade me that you have
been and set me down. Travel is my addiction.

He said this is the only time we'll meet and all
we'll know about each other. I want to show
you something magnificent and true. There are
two old women sobbing in the olive tree. Black
angels with olive oil hearts are offering you
their handkerchiefs and snow water. The Police
and the judge are stampeding through the grove.

He trampled through my eyes, my throat,
my ears. Our hour was gone. He'd spoken
and fallen silent. Although I'd always been
obedient no one had told me to be quiet.

ICE DANCING

He skipped across the river in his last delight
leaping from one runway of ice to another
until one swung loose. The current carried
his boat downstream. He was its lonesome

hand. This was no spaceship hurtling to
heaven. Nor did he lay his little dog body
down on the struts of our canoe or succumb
to the muscled roots in the oak tree well.

The river was his currency, the ridged slab
his chosen ribs. The cold was his accomplice,
the night his icicle collar. He might have said,
I'll take the river and we'll meet at the strand

but he kept so much to himself even though
we had long been companions in the dark.

APRIL MORNING

You are living the life
you wanted as if you'd known
what that was but of course
you didn't so you'd groped
toward it feeling for what
you couldn't imagine, what
your hands couldn't tell you,
for what that shape could be.

This Sunday the rain turns cold
again and steady but the window
is slightly open and there is the vaguest
sense of bird song somewhere in the gaps
between the buildings because it's spring
the calendar says and the room where
you are reading is empty yet full
of what loves you and this is the day
that you were born.

INVENTORY

Night is a stockroom of spare parts
that refurbish the day: mufflers
for noise and fumes, spark plugs
to challenge the heart, and wipers
to brush the snow.

Let's say you had misplaced everything.
Your children's shoes forgotten
in a starless field, the deposit box
key left in the pocket of an abandoned
jacket in a high closet, and your jar
of marbles clinging to eternal
dust somewhere in the attic.

Night leads you by the hand
and that is how you discover
the small sneakers forgotten
in the middle of their game
and how you came to try
on that moth-eaten coat.
Under the radiator coils
you spot the agate,
incandescent in the velvet dark.

And the heart that had tired
inside its cell of ribs feels
a charge flop across the gap
and turns over in its chamber
like a speckled trout drumming its tail
on the bottom of your aluminum boat.

RED FLAG

I wanted to read your poems
when I woke up but they were caked
in blood. It was the night's blood
that splotched across your lines
and blotted out the words.

I wanted to surprise your poems
that were sleeping before dawn,
but they were masked
by the wounds the bullets opened.
It is the blood of slaughter.
and the blood of sheep.
It is our blood that is still seeping.

I wanted to read your poems
but they vanished and this red
flag unravels in their place.

GLORIOUS

If it was a short life
             it still shone.

If it was off-kilter
             it was profound somehow.

If it was blinkered
             it never completely lost

its sense of touch,
             its open-handed greeting.

The glory was partaking
             of the sun

however briefly or blindly
             or however many times

it flew apart the more
             you tried to hold it.

Notes

"Taking off the Vest" is based on the article "Boko Harm strapped suicide bombs to them. Somehow these teenage girls survived." by Dionne Searcey, *The New York Times* 10/25/17

"Breathing into the Book" includes lines from *The Asiatics* by Frederic Prokosch, 1935

"Between Víznar and Alfacar" borrows details from Federico García Lorca's poem "Reyerta" translated by Robert Bly as "The Quarrel," page 125-127 "Lorca & Jiménez" Beacon Press 1997

Jonathan Wells is the author of two previous collections of poetry with Four Way Books: *Train Dance* (2011) and *The Man with Many Pens* (2015). His poems have appeared in *The New Yorker, Ploughshares, AGNI, Bennington Review* and many other journals. He is a co-editor of the New World Translation Series with Christopher Merrill and lives in New York.

Publication of this book was made possible by grants and donations. We are also grateful to those individuals who participated in our 2020 Build a Book Program. They are:

Anonymous (14), Robert Abrams, Nancy Allen, Maggie Anderson, Sally Ball, Matt Bell, Laurel Blossom, Adam Bohannon, Lee Briccetti, Therese Broderick, Jane Martha Brox, Christopher Bursk, Liam Callanan, Anthony Cappo, Carla & Steven Carlson, Paul & Brandy Carlson, Renee Carlson, Cyrus Cassells, Robin Rosen Chang, Jaye Chen, Edward W. Clark, Andrea Cohen, Ellen Cosgrove, Peter Coyote, Janet S. Crossen, Kim & David Daniels, Brian Komei Dempster, Matthew DeNichilo, Carl Dennis, Patrick Donnelly, Charles Douthat, Morgan Driscoll, Lynn Emanuel, Monica Ferrell, Elliot Figman, Laura Fjeld, Michael Foran, Jennifer Franklin, Sarah Freligh, Helen Fremont & Donna Thagard, Reginald Gibbons, Jean & Jay Glassman, Ginny Gordon, Lauri Grossman, Naomi Guttman & Jonathan Mead, Mark Halliday, Beth Harrison, Jeffrey Harrison, Page Hill Starzinger, Deming Holleran, Joan Houlihan, Thomas & Autumn Howard, Elizabeth Jackson, Christopher Johanson, Voki Kalfayan, Maeve Kinkead, David Lee, Jen Levitt, Howard Levy, Owen Lewis, Jennifer Litt, Sara London & Dean Albarelli, David Long, James Longenbach, Excelsior Love, Ralph & Mary Ann Lowen, Jacquelyn Malone, Donna Masini, Catherine McArthur, Nathan McClain, Richard McCormick, Victoria McCoy, Ellen McCulloch-Lovell, Judith McGrath, Debbie & Steve Modzelewski, Rajiv Mohabir, James T. F. Moore, Beth Morris, John Murillo & Nicole Sealey, Michael & Nancy Murphy, Maria Nazos, Kimberly Nunes, Bill O'Brien, Susan Okie & Walter Weiss, Rebecca Okrent, Sam Perkins, Megan Pinto, Kyle Potvin, Glen Pourciau, Kevin Prufer, Barbara Ras, Victoria Redel, Martha Rhodes, Paula Rhodes, Paula Ristuccia, George & Nancy Rosenfeld, M. L. Samios, Peter & Jill Schireson, Rob Schlegel, Roni & Richard Schotter, Jane Scovell, Andrew Seligsohn & Martina Anderson, James & Nancy Shalek, Soraya Shalforoosh, Peggy Shinner, Dara-Lyn Shrager, Joan Silber, Emily Sinclair, James Snyder & Krista Fragos, Alice St. Claire-Long,

Megan Staffel, Bonnie Stetson, Yerra Sugarman, Dorothy Tapper Goldman, Marjorie & Lew Tesser, Earl Teteak, Parker & Phyllis Towle, Pauline Uchmanowicz, Rosalynde Vas Dias, Connie Voisine, Valerie Wallace, Doris Warriner, Ellen Doré Watson, Martha Webster & Robert Fuentes, Calvin Wei, Bill Wenthe, Allison Benis White, Michelle Whittaker, and Ira Zapin.